Problem Solving, Communication, and Reasoning

Estimation and Logical Reasoning

10?
100?
1000?

HOW MANY FISH?

grade
4

Carole Greenes
Linda Schulman Dacey
Rika Spungin

Dale Seymour Publications®
White Plains, New York

DALE
SEYMOUR
PUBLICATIONS®

This book is published by Dale Seymour Publications®,
an imprint of Addison Wesley Longman, Inc.

Dale Seymour Publications
10 Bank Street
White Plains, New York 10602
Customer Service: 800-872-1100

Managing Editor: Catherine Anderson
Senior Editor: John Nelson
Project Editor: Mali Apple
Production/Manufacturing Director: Janet Yearian
Sr. Production/Manufacturing Coordinator: Fiona Santoianni
Design Director: Phyllis Aycock
Cover and Interior Illustrations: Jared Lee
Text and Cover Design: Tracey Munz
Composition and Computer Graphics: Alan Noyes

Order number 21876
ISBN 0-7690-0018-5

This Book Is Printed
On Recycled Paper

1 2 3 4 5 6 7 8 9 10-ML-03 02 01 00 99

contents

Introduction

Why Was *Hot Math Topics* Developed?

The *Hot Math Topics* series was developed for several reasons:

- to offer students practice and mainte-nance of previously learned skills and concepts
- to enhance problem solving and mathematical reasoning abilities
- to build literacy skills
- to nurture collaborative learning behaviors

Practicing and maintaining concepts and skills

Although textbooks and core curriculum materials do treat the topics explored in this series, their treatment is often limited by the lesson format and the page size. As a consequence, there are often not enough opportunities for students to practice newly acquired concepts and skills related to the topics, or to connect the topics to other content areas. *Hot Math Topics* provides the necessary practice and mathematical connections.

Similarly, core instructional programs often do not do a very good job of helping students maintain their skills. Although textbooks do include reviews of previously learned material, they are frequently limited to sidebars or boxed-off areas on one or two pages in each chapter, with four or five exercises in each box. Each set of problems is intended only as a sampling of previously taught topics, rather than as a complete review. In the selection and placement of the review exercises, little or no attention is given to levels of complexity of the problems. By contrast, *Hot Math Topics* targets specific topics and gives students more experience with concepts and skills related to them. The problems are sequenced by difficulty, allowing students to hone their skills. And, because they are not tied to specific lessons, the problems can be used at any time.

Enhancing problem solving and mathematical reasoning abilities

Hot Math Topics present students with situations in which they may use a variety of problem solving strategies, including

- designing and conducting experiments to generate or collect data
- guessing, checking, and revising guesses
- organizing data in lists or tables in order to identify patterns and relationships
- choosing appropriate computational algorithms and deciding on a sequence of computations
- using inverse operations in "work backward" solution paths

For their solutions, students are also required to bring to bear various methods of reasoning, including

- deductive reasoning
- inductive reasoning
- proportional reasoning

For example, to solve clue-type problems, students must reason deductively and make inferences about mathematical rela-tionships in order to generate candidates for the solutions and to home in on those that meet all of the problem's conditions.

To identify and continue a pattern and then write a rule for finding the next term in that pattern, students must reason inductively.

To compute unit prices and convert measurement units, students must reason proportionally.

To estimate or compare magnitudes of numbers, or to determine the type of number appropriate for a given situation, students must apply their number sense skills.

Building communication and literacy skills

Hot Math Topics offers students opportunities to write and talk about mathematical ideas. For many problems, students must describe their solution paths, justify their solutions, give their opinions, or write or tell stories.

Some problems have multiple solution methods. With these problems, students may have to compare their methods with those of their peers and talk about how their approaches are alike and different.

Other problems have multiple solutions, requiring students to confer to be sure they have found all possible answers.

Nurturing collaborative learning behaviors

Several of the problems can be solved by students working together. Some are designed specifically as partner problems. By working collaboratively, students can develop expertise in posing questions that call for clarification or verification, brainstorming solution strategies, and following another person's line of reasoning.

What Is in *Estimation and Logical Reasoning*?

This book contains 100 problems and tasks that focus on estimation and logical reasoning. The mathematics content, the mathematical connections, the problem solving strategies, and the communication skills that are emphasized are described below.

Mathematics content

The estimation and logical reasoning problems and tasks require students to

- estimate sums, differences, products, and quotients
- estimate number, length, area, capacity, mass, and time
- choose the best estimate
- make predictions
- continue and generalize patterns
- identify function rules
- use deductive, inductive, and proportional reasoning to solve problems
- identify relationships in maps, bar graphs, scatter plots, scale drawings, and Venn diagrams
- identify and describe similarities among elements in a group
- use number sense and measurement sense to match numbers and units to given situations
- round numbers to the nearest hundred, thousand, ten thousand, and dollar
- compute to solve problems

Mathematical connections

In these problems and tasks, connections are made to these other topic areas:

- arithmetic
- algebra

- geometry
- graphs
- measurement
- number theory
- probability

Problem solving strategies

Estimation and Logical Reasoning problems and tasks offer students opportunities to use one or more of several problem solving strategies.

- **Formulate Questions:** When data are presented in displays or text form, students must pose one or more questions that can be answered using the given data.
- **Complete Stories:** When confronted with an incomplete story, students must supply the missing information and then check that the story makes sense.
- **Organize Information:** To ensure that all possible solution candidates for a problem are considered, students may have to organize information by drawing a picture, making a list, or constructing a chart or a logic table.
- **Guess, Check, and Revise:** In some problems, students have to identify candidates for the solution and then check whether those candidates match the conditions of the problem. If the conditions are not satisfied, other possible solutions must be generated and verified.
- **Identify and Continue Patterns:** To identify the next term or terms in a sequence, students have to recognize the relationship between successive terms and then generalize that relationship.
- **Use Logic:** Students have to reason deductively, from clues, to make infer-

ences about the solution to a problem. They must reason proportionately to determine which of two buys is better. They have to reason inductively to continue numeric and shape patterns.

Communication skills

Problems and tasks in *Estimation and Logical Reasoning* are designed to stimulate communication. As part of the solution process, students may have to

- describe their thinking steps
- describe patterns and rules
- find alternate solution methods and solution paths
- identify other possible answers
- formulate problems for classmates to solve
- compare estimates, solutions, and methods with classmates
- make drawings to clarify mathematical relationships

These communication skills are enhanced when students interact with one another and with the teacher. By communicating both orally and in writing, students develop their understanding and use of the language of mathematics.

How Can *Hot Math Topics* Be Used?

The problems may be used as practice of newly learned concepts and skills, as maintenance of previously learned ideas, and as enrichment experiences for early finishers or more advanced students.

They may be used in class or assigned for homework. If used during class, they may be selected to complement lessons dealing with a specific topic or assigned every week as a means of keeping skills alive and well.

Because the problems often require the application of various problem solving strategies and reasoning methods, they may also form the basis of whole-class lessons whose goals are to develop expertise with specific problem solving strategies or methods.

The problems, which are sequenced from least to most difficult, may be used by students working in pairs or on their own. The selection of problems may be made by the teacher or the students based on their needs or interests. If the plan is for students to choose problems, you may wish to copy individual problems onto card stock and laminate them, and establish a problem card file.

To facilitate record keeping, a Management Chart is provided on page 6. The chart can be duplicated so that there is one for each student. As a problem is completed, the space corresponding to that problem's number may be shaded. An Award Certificate is included on page 6 as well.

How Can Student Performance Be Assessed?

Estimation and Logical Reasoning problems and tasks provide you with opportunities to assess students'

- estimation ability
- number sense

- logical reasoning methods
- computation abilities
- problem solving abilities
- communication skills

Observations

Keeping anecdotal records helps you to remember important information you gain as you observe students at work. To make observations more manageable, limit each observation to a group of from four to six students or to one of the areas noted above. You may find that using index cards facilitates the recording process.

Discussions

Many of the *Estimation and Logical Reasoning* problems and tasks allow for multiple answers or may be solved in a variety of ways. This built-in richness motivates students to discuss their work with one another. Small groups or class discussions are appropriate. As students share their approaches to the problems, you will gain additional insights into their content knowledge, mathematical reasoning, and communication abilities.

Scoring responses

You may wish to holistically score students' responses to the problems and tasks. The simple scoring rubric below uses three levels: high, medium, and low.

High	Medium	Low
• Solution demonstrates that the student knows the concepts and skills.	• Solution demonstrates that the student has some knowledge of the concepts and skills.	• Solution shows that the student has little or no grasp of the concepts and skills.
• Solution is complete and thorough.	• Solution is complete.	• Solution is incomplete or contains major errors.
• Student communicates effectively.	• Student communicates somewhat clearly.	• Student does not communicate effectively.

Portfolios

Having students store their responses to the problems in *Hot Math Topics* portfolios allows them to see improvement in their work over time. You may want to have them choose examples of their best responses for inclusion in their permanent portfolios, accompanied by explanations as to why each was chosen.

Students and the assessment process

Involving students in the assessment process is central to the development of their abilities to reflect on their own work, to understand the assessment standards to which they are held accountable, and to take ownership for their own learning. Young children may find the reflective process difficult, but with your coaching, they can develop such skills.

Discussion may be needed to help students better understand your standards for performance. Ask students such questions as, "What does it mean to communicate *clearly*?" "What is a *complete* response?"

Participation in peer-assessment tasks will also help students to better understand the performance standards. In pairs or small groups, students can review each other's responses and offer feedback. Opportunities to revise work may then be given.

What Additional Materials Are Needed?

Number cubes, a stopwatch or a clock with a second hand, a metric scale, grid paper, rulers and meter sticks, a dictionary, paper bags, newspapers, and a liter container are required for solving some of the problems in *Estimation and Logical Reasoning*. Cubes and calculators may also be helpful.

Management Chart

Name _____

When a problem or task is completed, shade the box with that number.

1	2	3	4	5	6	7	8	9	10
11	12	13	14	15	16	17	18	19	20
21	22	23	24	25	26	27	28	29	30
31	32	33	34	35	36	37	38	39	40
41	42	43	44	45	46	47	48	49	50
51	52	53	54	55	56	57	58	59	60
61	62	63	64	65	66	67	68	69	70
71	72	73	74	75	76	77	78	79	80
81	82	83	84	85	86	87	88	89	90
91	92	93	94	95	96	97	98	99	100

Award Certificate

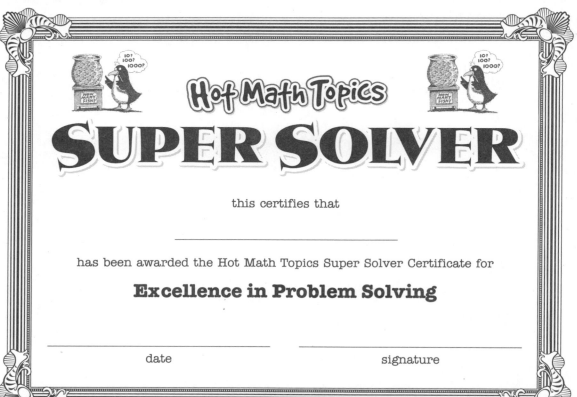

Hot Math Topics

SUPER SOLVER

this certifies that

_____

has been awarded the Hot Math Topics Super Solver Certificate for

Excellence in Problem Solving

_____   _____
date   signature

Problems and Tasks

There is more than 1 chip in each box.

There are fewer than 10 chips in each box.

Two of the boxes have the same number of chips.

The total number of chips in the boxes is 15.

Box A has the most chips.

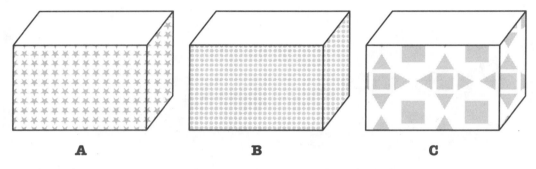

A   B   C

How many chips are in Box A? Box B? Box C?

Find another answer.

- -

Don't count the dots.

How many dots do you think there are?

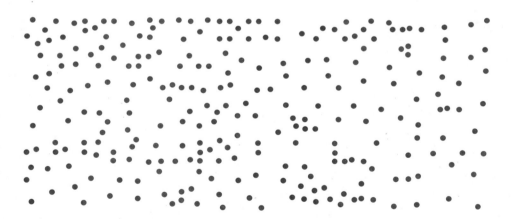

Draw a ring around a group of 10 dots.

Estimate again.

Explain how you estimated.

The faces of a number cube are labeled with 1, 2, 3, 4, 5, and 6 dots.

You will toss the cube 72 times.

Predict the number of times you think you will get 3 on the top face.

Prediction: _____

Now toss a number cube 72 times.

Count the number of times you get 3.

Experiment: _____

Why is there a difference between your prediction and the results of your experiment?

- -

Make up a rule. Use your rule to sort these shapes into two sets.

The sets must have different numbers of shapes.

Which shapes are in each set?

Make up another rule.

Use your rule to sort the shapes into two sets, with the same number of shapes in each set.

Which shapes are in each set?

Mr. Gardner planted flower beds of tulips, roses, daisies, and marigolds.

The tulips are planted directly between the roses and the daisies.

The marigolds are planted just to the left of the daisies.

Make a drawing to show the order of the flower beds.

----

penny	nickel	dime	quarter
3 grams	5 grams	2 grams	6 grams

You have 7 coins.

Together they weigh about 28 grams.

What is the most money you could have?

What is the least money you could have?

©Addison Wesley Longman, Inc./Published by Dale Seymour Publications®

©Addison Wesley Longman, Inc./Published by Dale Seymour Publications®

Estimate the area inside the curve.

Describe your estimation method.

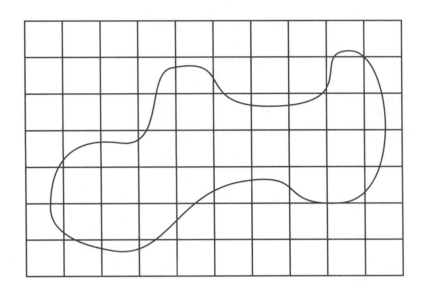

- -

8

Fill in the measurement units that make the most sense.

Julius is 10 _____ old. He is 56 _____ tall.

He walks $1\frac{1}{2}$ _____ to school each day.

It takes him about 25 _____ to get to school.

His brother Mario is 3 _____ tall.

Mario goes to preschool for $2\frac{1}{2}$ _____ each day.

Talk about your choices with a classmate.

©Addison Wesley Longman, Inc./Published by Dale Seymour Publications®

9

Get a newspaper.

Find two places where an estimate is used.

Why do you think an estimate was used instead of an exact number?

- -

Jeff, Paul, Sara, and Lelia each baked something for the bake sale.

10

Who baked which item?

- Jeff did not bake muffins.
- One of the girls baked the brownies.
- Sara's item cost more than Lelia's but less than Paul's.

Jeff baked _____ . **Paul baked** _____ .

Sara baked _____ . **Lelia baked** _____ .

4 9

28 5

Use the numbers shown.

Write one number on each line to complete the story.

The story must make sense.

A Ping-Pong table is _____ feet long and _____ feet wide.

Its length is _____ feet longer than its width.

The perimeter of the table is _____ feet.

- -

Rachel got a sweater from each of her friends, Hana, Megan, and Diedre.

She forgot who gave her the red sweater, the blue sweater, and the green sweater.

Her mother said, "Neither Hana nor Diedre gave you the green sweater. Diedre did not give you the red sweater."

"Now I know who gave me each sweater!" said Rachel.

"Hana gave me the _____ sweater. Megan gave me the _____ sweater. Diedre gave me the _____ sweater."

©Addison Wesley Longman, Inc./Published by Dale Seymour Publications®

13

Roll-and-Score Rules

- Start with 100 points.

- Roll a number cube numbered 1 through 6.

- If the number is greater than 3, subtract 5 points from your score.

- If the number is equal to or less than 3, add 8 points to your score.

- Roll 12 times.

Before playing, predict what you think would be a likely score at the end of a game of Roll-and-Score.

Explain your thinking.

Play the game.

How does your score compare with your prediction?

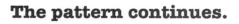

14

Columns

	A	B	C	D	E	F	G
Row 1	1	2	3	4	5	6	7
Row 2	8	9	10	11	12	13	14
Row 3	15	16	17	18	19	20	21
Row 4	22	23	24	25	26	27	28
Row 5	29	30	31	32	33	34	35
Row 6							
Row 7							
Row 8							

The pattern continues.

In which row and column is 60?

©Addison Wesley Longman, Inc./Published by Dale Seymour Publications®

Write a rule in words.

Tell how to use the building number to find the number of cubes in each building.

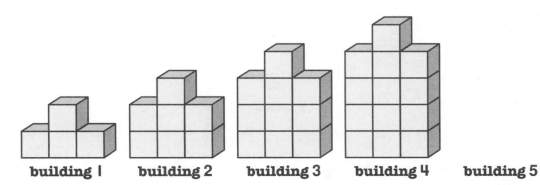

building 1   building 2   building 3   building 4   building 5

Compare your rule with a friend's rule.

Use your rule and your friend's rule.

How many cubes are in building 10?

- -

Books Read by Club Members

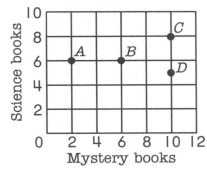

Name the person represented by each dot.

- Andrew read twice as many mystery books as science books.

- Joy and Nathan read the same number of science books.

- Zack read 6 more books than Nathan read.

A is _____ .   **B** is _____ .

C is _____ .   **D** is _____ .

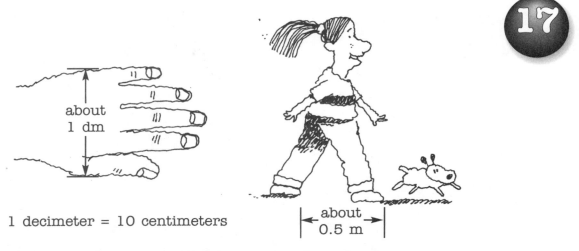

1 decimeter = 10 centimeters

Use the pictures to help you estimate the

- length and width of a book.
- length of your classroom.
- height of a chair.

Using exactly 8 triangles like this, which of the shapes shown below can you make?

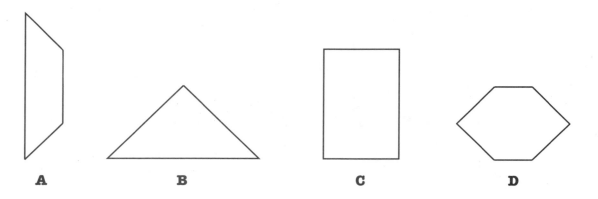

A   B   C   D

What did you do to figure it out?

©Addison Wesley Longman, Inc./Published by Dale Seymour Publications®

60
63
57
48

Use the numbers shown.

Find each person's height.

Jin Lee: "I am not the tallest or the shortest.
I am _____ inches tall."

Mark: "I am 1 foot 3 inches shorter than Lisa.
I am _____ inches tall."

Lisa: "I am $\frac{1}{2}$ foot taller than Benita.
I am _____ inches tall."

Benita: "I am $\frac{1}{4}$ foot shorter than Jin Lee.
I am _____ inches tall."

- -

Tell how you think each person estimated.

Which technique do you think is better?

Why?

With 2 types of eyeglasses, 1 hat, and 2 kinds of mustaches, you can make 4 different disguises.

Suppose you want to make 18 different disguises.

What is the fewest number of different types of glasses, hats, and mustaches you will need?

glasses: _____   hats: _____   mustaches: _____

- -

What is * doing?

Describe the rule in words.

$$2 * 5 = 12 \qquad 7 * 3 = 13$$

$$10 * 6 = 22 \qquad 8 * 4 = 16$$

Fill in the circles.

$$6 * 6 = \bigcirc \qquad 1 * 8 = \bigcirc$$

$$\bigcirc * 9 = 18 \qquad 3 * \bigcirc = 27$$

Which pattern will fold to make the cube?

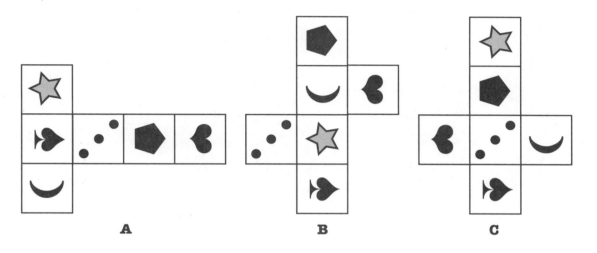

A   B   C

- -

1   5

3   7

Use each digit once to write a number that

- rounded to the nearest thousand is 4000: _____
- rounded to the nearest thousand is 6000: _____
- rounded to the nearest hundred is 5100: _____
- rounded to the nearest hundred is 7400: _____
- rounded to the nearest ten is 3520: _____

The school bus travels from Charlotte to Mendon.

Estimate the distance the bus travels.

Tell how you made your estimate.

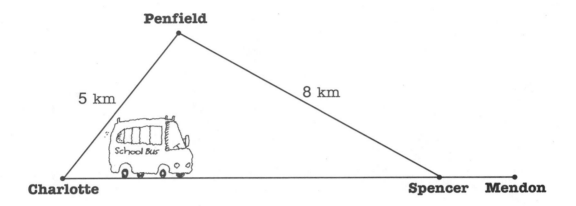

Make a list of possibilities.

- I am between 100 and 1000.

- All my digits are divisible by 3.

- Each digit is greater than or equal to the digit to its left.

Work with a partner.

Each of you fill a bag with things in your classroom.

Stop when you think the bag weighs 1 kilogram.

Weigh each bag.

Whose estimate is closer to 1 kilogram?

Do it again.

Whose estimate is closer to 1 kilogram?

Which is the better buy?

| 3 pounds $4.98 | 2 pounds $3.60 |

Tell how you decided.

Scales A and B are balanced.

To balance scale C, how many **do you need to put on the empty pan?**

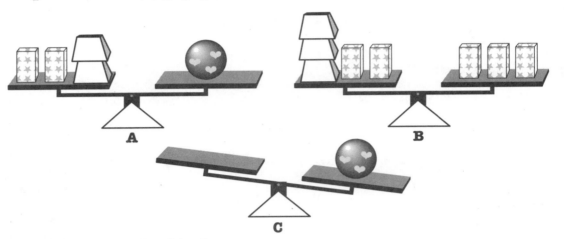

A

B

C

Tell how you decided.

Compare your explanation with a classmate's.

- -

28

454

5

240

140

Use the numbers shown.

Complete the story.

The story must make sense.

The full jar of jelly weighs _____ grams.

The weight of the jelly is about half that of the full jar, or about _____ grams.

To make a peanut butter and jelly sandwich, you use about _____ grams of jelly.

To make _____ peanut butter and jelly sandwiches, you use about _____ grams of jelly.

What is ✳ doing?

Describe the rule in words.

$2 ✳ 6 = 12$ $8 ✳ 1 = 25$

$5 ✳ 0 = 15$ $10 ✳ 9 = 39$

Fill in the circles.

$1 ✳ 7 =$ ◯ $4 ✳$ ◯ $= 15$

$6 ✳ 2 =$ ◯   ◯ $✳ 9 = 30$

Compare your answer with your classmates' answers.

- -

Victor's Pizzeria

Special!
Buy one pizza for $9.95.
Get a second for $5.95.

Reva has $4.50.

José has $3.75.

Marcus has $5.10.

Estimate to answer this question: Together, do they have enough money to buy 2 pizzas?

Explain.

Isabel does not like apple juice.

Lin likes only apple juice and orange juice.

Jerome does not like grape juice or orange juice.

If there is one box of each type of juice, which kind will each person choose?

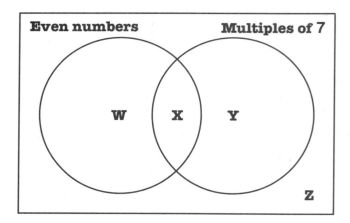

Name three numbers that fit in each of the four areas.

W: _____

X: _____

Y: _____

Z: _____

Wait one minute, please!

Work with a partner.

Your partner says "Start" while watching the second hand of a clock.

When you think 1 minute has passed, say "Stop!"

Compare your estimate with the actual length of time.

Do this activity four more times.

Do your estimates improve as you repeat the experiment?

- -

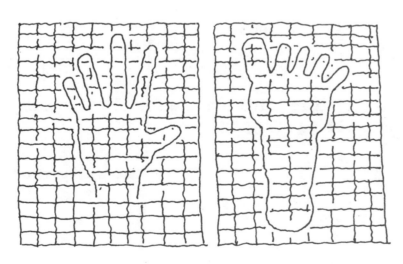

Use two pieces of grid paper.

On one piece, trace around your hand.

On the other piece, trace around your foot.

About how many times greater is the area of your foot than the area of your hand?

How did you figure it out?

37

Estimate the cost of

- 1 muffin
- 1 piece of carrot cake
- 1 fruit bar

Quilt Squares

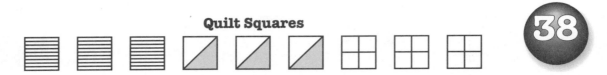

38

Use the clues to figure out how the 9 quilt squares are arranged on the quilt grid.

Clues

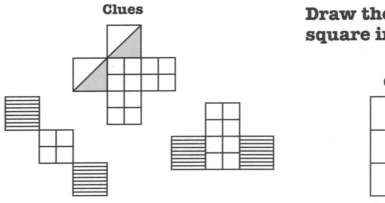

Draw the pattern on each square in the quilt grid.

Quilt Grid

39

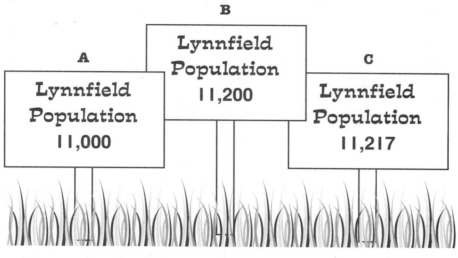

A
Lynnfield
Population
11,000

B
Lynnfield
Population
11,200

C
Lynnfield
Population
11,217

On January 1, the population of Lynnfield was 11,217.

You want to put up a permanent sign to show the population.

Which sign would you use? Why?

- -

1600   62.7   132

15   1888

40

Use the numbers shown to complete the story.

The story must make sense.

There were _____ presidents before President Lincoln.

The land area of Washington, D.C., is _____ square miles.

The Washington Monument first opened to the public in _____ .

The White House is located at _____ Pennsylvania Avenue.

The number of rooms in the White House is _____ .

Estimate to find the perimeter of each figure.

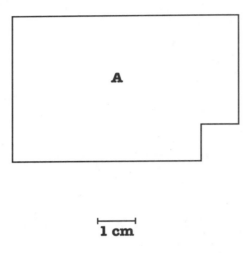

1 cm

- -

Fill in the triangles and circles to make two problems with the same answer.

Do not use any zeros.

$$\begin{array}{cccc} \triangle & \triangle & \triangle & \triangle \\ - \quad \triangle & \triangle & \triangle & \triangle \\ \hline 2 & 4 & 7 & 8 \end{array}$$

$$\begin{array}{cccc} \bigcirc & \bigcirc & \bigcirc & \bigcirc \\ - \quad \bigcirc & \bigcirc & \bigcirc & \bigcirc \\ \hline 2 & 4 & 7 & 8 \end{array}$$

14 ³⁰ 20 ¹² 6

Each kind of block weighs a different number of pounds.

Which of the numbers above could be the weight of each block?

 = _____ pounds

 = _____ pounds

 = _____ pounds

- -

Keenan, Bryan, and Vanessa work for the Eager Lawn Mowing Company.

This weekend they each mowed 4 lawns and worked for 12 hours.

- Keenan earned $250.

- Bryan earned $72 for each lawn he mowed.

- Vanessa received $22 an hour.

Estimate to find who earned the most money.

Describe your thinking steps.

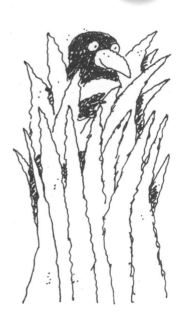

At 3:00 P.M. Blake heard a rumor.

After exactly 10 minutes, he told it to 3 people.

After exactly 10 more minutes, each of those
3 people told 3 new people.

Assume this rumor telling continues.

How many people will have heard the rumor
by 3:41 P.M.?

- -

A $5 bill is 6 inches long.

About how many $5 bills laid end-to-end would you
need to make a border for the classroom floor?

Describe your method for estimating.

Estimate.

About how many sheets of notebook paper would you need to cover the classroom floor?

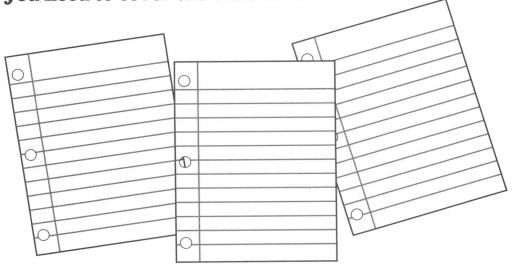

How did you make your estimate?

- -

You have one 1-inch strip, one 3-inch strip, and one 9-inch strip.

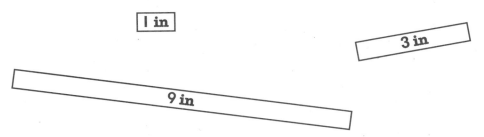

How can you use the strips to measure lengths of

- 2 inches?
- 4 inches?
- 5 inches?
- 6 inches?

Draw pictures to show how you could make each measurement.

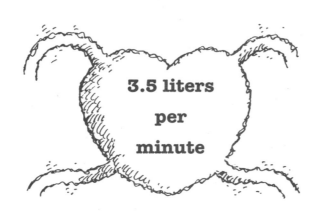

3.5 liters per minute

Your heart pumps about 3.5 liters of blood every minute.

Estimate how much blood your heart pumps in one day.

Now use a calculator to compute the amount of blood your heart pumps in one day.

How close is your estimate to your calculation?

- -

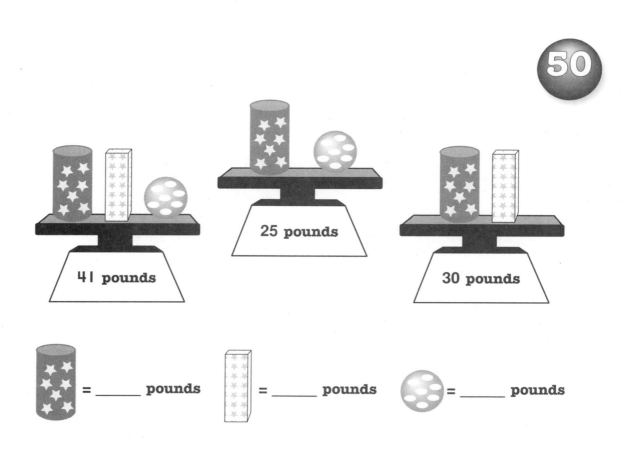

25 pounds

41 pounds

30 pounds

= _____ pounds   = _____ pounds   = _____ pounds

The soccer team washed cars and sold sports mugs to raise money for new uniforms.

They washed 58 cars at $6 each.

They sold 21 mugs for $8 each.

All the supplies were donated.

Estimate: Has the team raised enough money to buy $500 worth of uniforms?

Explain.

51

- -

The same letters represent the same digits.

52

$$\begin{array}{r} AB \\ + BB \\ \hline DDC \end{array}$$

A = _____   B = _____   C = _____   D = _____

$$\begin{array}{r} RS \\ + RR \\ \hline TSR \end{array}$$

R = _____   S = _____   T = _____

The same letters represent the same digits.

Assume there is no regrouping.

What numbers are possible for the letter O?

Tell why you think so.

$$\begin{array}{r} ONE \\ + ONE \\ \hline TWO \end{array}$$

Find another solution to the problem.

- -

Use the clues to find the number.

Clues

- It is a multiple of 4.
- It is not evenly divisible by 10.
- When you divide by 8, there is a remainder of 4.
- It is not equal to 139 + 145.

©Addison Wesley Longman, Inc./Published by Dale Seymour Publications®

Assume the pattern continues.

In what row will the middle number be 50?

Row 1   /2\

Row 2   /2\ /4\ /2\

Row 3   /2\ /4\ /6\ /4\ /2\

Row 4 /2\ /4\ /6\ /8\ /6\ /4\ /2\

Row 5 /2\ /4\ /6\ /8\ /10\ /8\ /6\ /4\ /2\

Make up 5 other questions about the pattern.

Given them to a friend to answer.

- -

Ring two numbers in each box.

Their difference must be in the range.

2900	2010
1725	1500
	3600

Range: 200–400

579	540
600	710
	910

Range: 25–100

45	908
938	19
	720

Range: 900–1000

Arno, Benita, Chan, and David
have different teachers.

The teachers are Ms. Apple,
Mr. Berg, Ms. Chan, and Mr. Dolby.

Who is each student's teacher?

Facts

- No student's first name begins with the same letter
  as the teacher's last name.

- Benita and Chan do not have Ms. Apple.

- Arno does not have Mr. Berg.

- Benita's teacher is a woman.

Student	Arno	Benita	Chan	David
Teacher	_____	_____	_____	_____

- -

Pick pairs of numbers from the sign.

Estimate their sums to complete the
statements.

Use each number once.

The sum of _____ and _____ is between
5000 and 6000.

The sum of _____ and _____ is between
7000 and 8000.

The sum of _____ and _____ is between
8000 and 9000.

The sum of _____ and _____ is between
9000 and 10,000.

4279	4805
2900	
3185	4590
96	1999
8000	

©Addison Wesley Longman, Inc./Published by Dale Seymour Publications®

**Find something in your classroom that satisfies
each of the following.**

1. Is about 1 meter long

2. Weighs about 1 kilogram

3. Has a perimeter of about 150 centimeters

4. Has a capacity of about 1 liter

Item	Estimate	Actual Measurement	Difference
	1 m		
	1 kg		
	150 cm		
	1 liter		

Check your estimates by measuring your choices.

Which estimate is closest to the actual measurement?

- -

Write the names of the cities on the map.

- At a speed of 45 miles per hour, the drive
  from Oceanside to Riverdale would take 3 hours.

- The distance from Oceanside to Harbortown is
  twice the distance from Harbortown to Lakewood.

- The distance from Bayview to Harbortown is
  2 miles greater than the distance from Bayview
  to Riverdale.

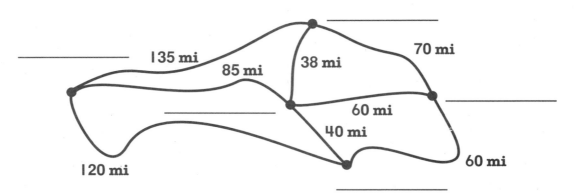

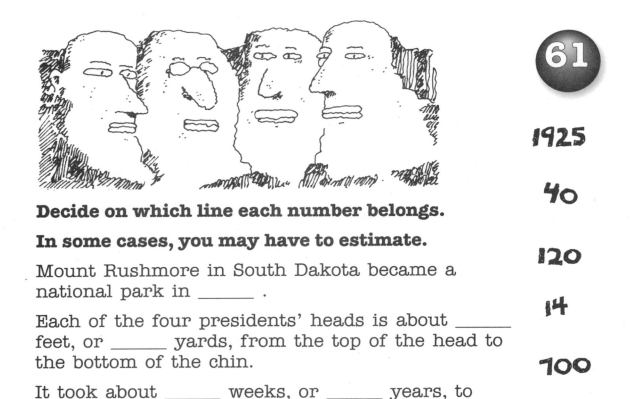

61

1925

40

120

14

700

Decide on which line each number belongs.

In some cases, you may have to estimate.

Mount Rushmore in South Dakota became a national park in _____ .

Each of the four presidents' heads is about _____ feet, or _____ yards, from the top of the head to the bottom of the chin.

It took about _____ weeks, or _____ years, to carve the heads.

- -

Which shape is the mystery shape?

62

- All of its sides are congruent.

- Its perimeter is 12 centimeters.

- You can fold it in half to make two triangles.

- It has 4 lines of symmetry.

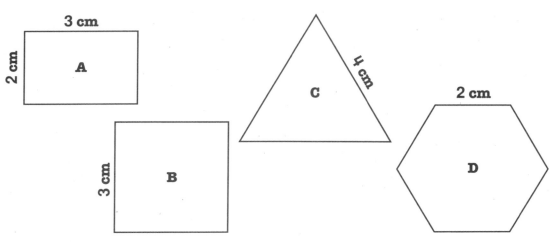

63

Which brand is the better buy?

Give two ways to tell.

- -

All of these are flumpers.

64

None of these are flumpers.

Which one of these is a flumper?

   A   B   C   D

Describe a flumper.

Play this game with a friend. Take turns.

Use different colors of crayons.

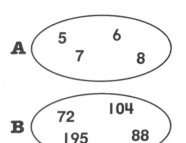

A (5   6   7   8)

B (72   104   195   88)

Playing Board

1200	540	500	420
600	350	1400	700
1600	560	720	800
490	630	1000	450

Choose one number from A and one number from B.

Estimate their product.

Color the product on the Playing Board.

The winner is the first to get 4 in a row, →↓ ↘ or ↗.

- -

Estimate to find the length of each line.

⊢—⊣
1 cm

///////////////////////////////////// _____ cm

/////////// _____ mm

/// _____ mm

///////////////////////// _____ cm

//////////////////// _____ mm

A number is subtracted from 372.

The difference is less than 100.

What do you know about the number?

Another number is divided by 8.

The quotient is greater than 125.

What do you know about the number?

- -

Use the clues to find the number.

Put the numbers in the boxes.

Clues

- The digits in the number are 2, 3, 6, 8, and 9.
- The digit in the ones place is 5 less than the digit in the hundreds place.
- When rounded to the nearest ten thousand, the number is 60,000.

Write your own clues for the number 27,346.

Give your problem to a friend to solve.

Pick the closest estimate for each problem. Explain your thinking.

Problem	Estimate
36,425 + 44,362	70,000 or 80,000
472 × 3	1200 or 1500
3323 ÷ 4	800 or 900
93,620 − 49,738	40,000 or 50,000

- -

Conduct a survey.

Ask 10 people which of these juices they like best.

Make a tally mark next to each juice chosen.

After your survey, predict: If you surveyed 1000 people, how many people would choose

- carrot juice? _____

- cranberry juice? _____

- apple juice? _____

- orange juice? _____

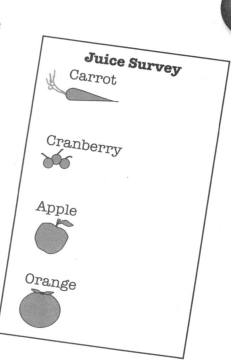

Juice Survey
Carrot
Cranberry
Apple
Orange

Use the facts.

Label each point with the name of the city.

Facts

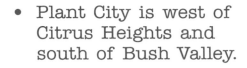

- Ferndale is east of Bush Valley and west of Orangevale.

- Stumptown is west of Plant City.

- Plant City is west of Citrus Heights and south of Bush Valley.

- Treetown is the farthest north. Citrus Heights is the farthest south.

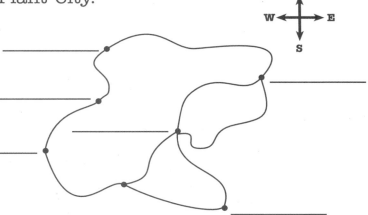

- -

The Long Bench in the Boston Public Garden is 65 feet long.

Two people need about $3\frac{1}{2}$ feet to sit comfortably on the bench.

About how many people could sit comfortably on the whole bench?

What did you do to decide?

Write numbers in the blanks so that the estimated sum, difference, and product are all 3600.

_____ + _____ is about 3600.

_____ − _____ is about 3600.

_____ × _____ is about 3600.

3600

- -

Put a number on each line to fit the facts.

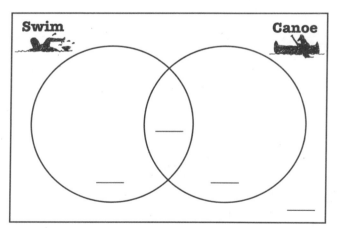

Facts

- There are 20 students altogether.

- Half of the students know how to swim and canoe.

- Five students can swim, but not canoe.

- Three students can canoe, but not swim.

Work with a partner.

Take turns doing the activities and timing them.

Estimate first, and then use a stopwatch to check.

1. How many seconds does it take you to find the product 8×236?

2. How many seconds does it take you to look up the word *mathematics* in the dictionary?

3. How many seconds does it take you to draw a line $6\frac{3}{4}$ inches long?

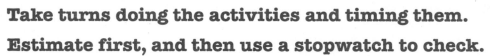

Activity	Estimates	Actual Values
1		
2		
3		

Work with a friend.

If all the students in your school lined up, how long would the line be?

Tell how you figured it out.

Barry, Sharel, Rachel, and Everett each have a different pet.

- Barry and Everett don't like cats.

- Sharel's pet runs away from dogs, mice, and rabbits.

- Rachel's pet is bigger than a mouse.

- Rachel and Barry took their pets to visit the owner of the dog.

Use the table to help you find out who owns the rabbit.

	Mouse	Cat	Rabbit	Dog
Barry		×		
Sharel				
Rachel				
Everett				

The × shows that Barry doesn't own the cat.

- -

Name the person represented by each dot.

- Elvin and Lindsay live the same number of miles from the museum.

- Carey lives farthest from the museum.

- Janet rode her bike to the museum.

- Lindsay walked and Elvin jogged to the museum.

A is _____ .   *B* is _____ .

C is _____ .   *D* is _____ .

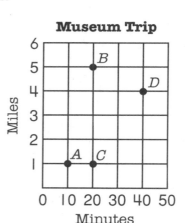

Museum Trip

©Addison Wesley Longman, Inc./Published by Dale Seymour Publications®

Mr. Chen leaves Brookview at 10:00 A.M.

He drives to Johnson City at an average speed of 60 miles per hour.

How many miles is he from Brookview when he is 2 hours from Johnson City?

Tell how you know.

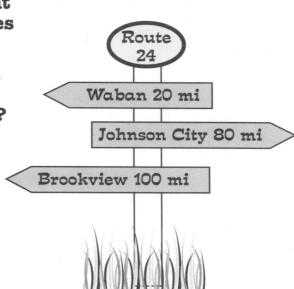

Put the greatest possible whole number in each shape. Put the same numbers in the same shapes.

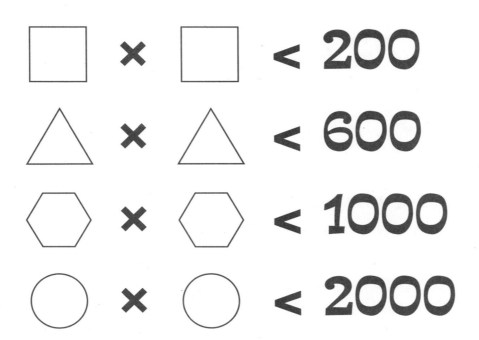

$$\square \times \square < 200$$

$$\triangle \times \triangle < 600$$

$$\hexagon \times \hexagon < 1000$$

$$\bigcirc \times \bigcirc < 2000$$

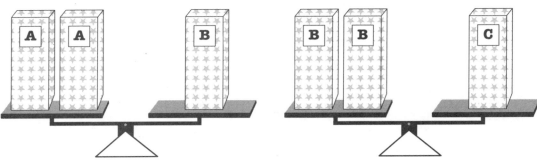

Which is heavier, A or C?

How many times heavier?

Tell how you know.

- -

Savanna saves $5.50 each week.

Will she be able to buy a bicycle for $275 after saving for one year?

Explain how you can use estimation to answer the question.

There are 25 students in the music club.

Eighteen of the students play an instrument.

Twelve of the students sing in the choir.

How many students play an instrument and also sing in the choir?

How many students only sing in the choir?

- -

There are 800 students in Canton Elementary School.

The bar graph shows the number of students in the computer club each year from 1996 through 1999.

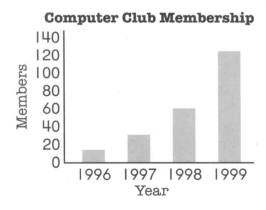

Computer Club Membership

About how many students do you think will be in the club in 2001?

How did you make your prediction?

Your heart beats about 70 times a minute.

Hani said, "That means my heart beats about 50,000 times in one day!"

Is Hani right?

Explain.

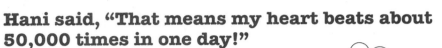

You multiply 2 numbers.

There are 4 digits in the product.

How many digits can there be in each factor?

Explain your thinking.

Give examples.

Carmen has a collection of pennies.

When she puts them in piles of 4, she has **2** left over.

When she puts them in piles of 5, she has **2** left over.

When she puts them in piles of 6, she has none left over.

What is the fewest number of pennies Carmen could have?

How did you figure it out?

- -

All of these are zippies.

  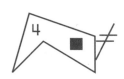 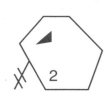

None of these are zippies.

 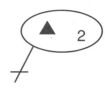 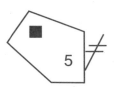 

Which of these are zippies? Why?

W	X	Y	Z

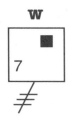 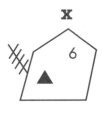 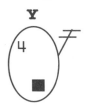 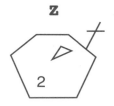

There are 24 people at the party.

There are twice as many females as males.

There are 5 times as many children as adults.

How many males are at the party?

How many children are at the party?

Find the populations of the largest cities in Michigan.

- To the nearest ten thousand, the populations of Warren and Flint round to the same number.

- Detroit has more than one million people.

- The population of Grand Rapids is 48,365 greater than the population of Flint.

If you don't live in Michigan, how do these populations compare with the largest cities in your state?

140,761
127,321
1,027,974
189,126
144,864

Detroit: _____

Flint: _____

Grand Rapids: _____

Lansing: _____

Warren: _____

There are about 250 new dollar bills in a stack 1 inch thick.

About how many feet high would a stack of 25,000 new one-dollar bills be?

Describe your thinking steps.

- -

Play Target Number with a friend.

- Use nine cards numbered 1 through 9.

| 1 | 2 | 3 | 4 | 5 | 6 | 7 | 8 | 9 |

- Shuffle the cards and place them face down.

- Turn over a card.

- Each player writes the number in a box on his or her playing card.

- Continue until all the number cards are used.

- Score: The number closer to each target scores 1 point.

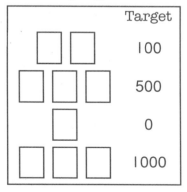

Player 1's Playing Card

	Target
☐ ☐	100
☐ ☐ ☐	500
☐	0
☐ ☐ ☐	1000

Player 2's Playing Card

	Target
☐ ☐	100
☐ ☐ ☐	500
☐	0
☐ ☐ ☐	1000

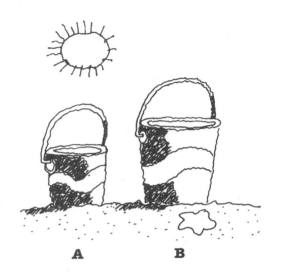

You have two pails.

Pail A holds 3 cups of sand.

Pail B holds 7 cups of sand.

How can you use the two pails to get exactly
5 cups of sand in pail B?

The number 9 is in row 2, column B.

The pattern continues.

In which row and column would you find 272?

	A	B	C	D	E
Row 5	21	22	23	24	25
Row 4	20	19	18	17	16
Row 3	11	12	13	14	15
Row 2	10	9	8	7	6
Row 1	1	2	3	4	5

©Addison Wesley Longman, Inc./Published by Dale Seymour Publications®

©Addison Wesley Longman, Inc./Published by Dale Seymour Publications®

95

3 RAZZLES = 2 DAZZLES

4 DAZZLES = 12 JAZZLES

2 RAZZLES = _____ JAZZLES

Tell how you found your answer.

- -

96

Fill in the blanks

Square is to cube as circle is to _____ .

3 is to 9 as 7 is to _____.

_____ is to _____ as _____ is to _____.

Compare your answers with a friend's answers.

Talk about your thinking.

The perimeter of the mystery rectangle is 32 feet.

The length of the mystery rectangle is 10 feet.

What is the area of the mystery rectangle?

- -

Work with a partner.

Measure your walking step.

Estimate: About how many steps would you take
to walk a mile?

How can you use one or both of these two
products to find the product 36 × 62?

$$36 \times 72 = 2592$$

$$36 \times 52 = 1872$$

Are the towers the same height?

Give two ways to decide.

Tower Z

Scale
1 inch = 120 feet

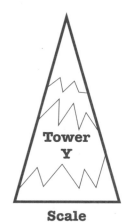

Tower Y

Scale
1 inch = 41 yards

Why are they the same height in the picture?

Answers

1. A, 9; B, 3; C, 3 or A, 7; B, 4; C, 4

2. Answers will vary. Students might estimate the number of groups of 10 and multiply. There are 260 dots.

3. Answers will vary. In the long run, the probability of getting 3 is $\frac{1}{6}$.

4. Possible rules: Circles; one set has 4 shapes; the other has 8 shapes (triangles and squares). Blue or green; one set has blue and green; the other has red and yellow (6 in each set).

5. marigolds, daisies, tulips, roses

6. The most is 97¢: 3 quarters, 2 dimes, 2 pennies. The least is 39¢: 1 quarter, 2 nickels, 4 pennies.

7. approximately 25 squares; Methods will vary.

8. years; inches; miles or kilometers; minutes; feet; hours

9. Answers will vary.

10. Jeff, bars; Paul, apple muffins; Sara, bran muffins; Lelia, brownies

11. 9, 5, 4, 28

12. red, green, blue

13. Answers will vary. As outcomes are equally likely, it is reasonable to expect to roll 6 numbers > 3 ($6 \times 5 = 30$) and 6 numbers ≤ 3 ($6 \times 8 = 48$); then, $100 - 30 + 48 = 118$ points.

14. row 9, column D

15. Rules will vary; 31 cubes

16. A, Joy; B, Nathan; C, Zack; D, Andrew

17. Estimates will vary.

18. B and D; Explanations will vary.

19. 60, 48, 63, 57

20. Noah rounded to the nearest 10, $10 + 10 + 20 + 40 = 80$. Regina rounded to the nearest dollar, $10 + 14 + 22 + 43 = 89$. Which is better depends on the situation. Noah's technique makes easier mental arithmetic. Regina's gives a closer estimate, which may be important in a money situation.

21. 3, 3, 2 (in any order)

22. The ✳ is adding the first number to twice the second number; 18, 17, 0, 12

23. C

24. 3517, 3571, 3715, or 3751; 5713 or 5731; 5137; 7351; 3517

25. about 12 km; Explanations will vary.

26. 333, 336, 339, 366, 369, 399, 666, 669, 699, 999

28. 3 pounds for $4.98; Possible explanations:

    • Compare unit costs: $4.98 ÷ 3 ≈ $1.66 and $3.60 ÷ 2 = $1.80.

    • Find the cost of 6 pounds (6 is the LCM of 3 and 2): $2 \times \$4.98 = \$9.96$; $3 \times \$3.60 = \$10.80$.

29. 8; Explanations will vary.

30. 454, 240, 28, 5, 140

31. The ✳ is multiplying the first number by 3 and adding the product to the second number; 10, 3, 20, 7

32. no; The pizza will cost about $10 + 6 = \$16$, and they have only about $4 + 4 + 5 = \$13$.

33. Jerome, apple; Isabel, grape; Lin, orange

34. Possible answer: W, 2, 4, 8;
    X, 14, 28, 42; Y, 7, 21, 35; Z, 1, 3, 5

36. Answers will vary.

37. Possible answer: 40¢, 30¢, 35¢

38. Possible answer:

39. Answers will vary. A or B would allow
    for people to move in and out of the
    city and the number would remain a
    good estimate. If the population is
    increasing, 11,200 is better; if it is
    decreasing, 11,000 is better.

40. 15, 62.7, 1888, 1600, 132

41. Estimates will vary; the perimeters
    are A, 20 cm; B, 16 cm; C, 22 cm.

42. Answers will vary.

43. 12, 20, 14

44. Bryan; Explanations will vary.

45. 121 people

46. Estimates and methods will vary.

47. Estimates and methods will vary.

48.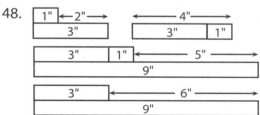

49. Estimates will vary; 5040 liters

50. 14, 16, 11

51. yes; Possible explanation: 60 × 6 = $360,
    20 × 8 = $160, and 360 + 160 = $520

52. Answers will vary. D is 1 because A +
    B and any regrouped 10 from B + B
    must add to 11; 46 + 66 = 112, 92 +
    22 = 114, 28 + 88 = 116, 74 + 44 =
    118. R = 5, S = 0, T = 1

53. 2 or 4; Possible explanation: O is
    even, as E + E = O. O can't be zero, as
    it's in the hundreds place. O can't be

6 or 8, as there is no regrouping. Thus
O can be 2 or 4; e.g., 231 + 231 = 462
and 432 + 432 = 864.

54. 292

55. row 25; Questions will vary.

56. 1500 and 1725 or 1725 and 2010; 579
    and 540 or 540 and 600; 19 and 938

57. Arno, Mr. Dolby; Benita, Ms. Chan;
    Chan, Mr. Berg; David, Ms. Apple

58. 3185 and 1999; 2900 and 4279;
    96 and 8000; 4805 and 4590

59. Answers will vary.

60.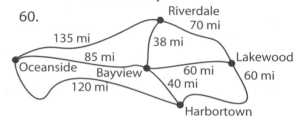

61. 1925, 120, 40, 700, 14

62. B

63. Drawing Board; Possible explana-
    tions:

    • Compare unit costs: Art's,
      $1.50 ÷ 6 = 25¢ each; Drawing
      Board, $2.00 ÷ 9 ≈ 22¢ each.

    • Find the cost of 18 pencils
      (18 is the LCM of 6 and 9):
      Art's, 3 × $1.50 = $4.50; Drawing
      Board, 2 × $2.00 = $4.00.

64. C; A flumper has a black polygon
    within a square within a circle. A line
    segment connects a corner of the
    black polygon to a corner of the
    square. Another connects a corner
    of the square to the circle.

66. Estimates will vary. The lengths are 8
    cm, 25 mm, 100 mm, 6 cm, 37.5 mm.

67. The first number is greater than 272;
    the second is greater than 1000.

68. 62,893; Clues will vary.

69. 80,000; 1500; 800; 40,000; Explanations will vary.

70. Predictions should be 100 times the results for 10 people.

71.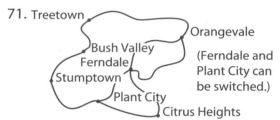
Treetown
Orangevale
Bush Valley
Ferndale
Stumptown
Plant City
Citrus Heights
(Ferndale and Plant City can be switched.)

72. about 36 people; Methods will vary.

73. Answers will vary.

74. from left to right: 5, 10, 3, 2

75. Answers will vary.

76. Answers and explanations will vary.

77. Rachel

78. A, Elvin; B, Carey; C, Lindsay; D, Janet

79. 60 miles; He is $60 \times 2 = 120$ miles from Johnson City. It is 180 miles from Brookview to Johnson City, and $180 - 120 = 60$ miles.

80. 14×14; 24×24; 31×31; 44×44

81. C; 4 times heavier; Possible explanations: If A is 10, then B is 20, so $C = 20 + 20 = 40$. Or, 2 B's equal 1 C, so B equals $\frac{1}{2}$ of C. Since $\frac{1}{2}$ of C equals 2 A's, 1 C equals 4 A's.

82. yes; Possible explanation: $\$5 \times 50$ weeks $= \$250$, and $\$1 \times 25$ weeks $= \$25$, and $\$250 + \$25 = \$275$.

83. 5 students; 7 students

84. Answers will vary. Students should note an increase of at least double in successive years.

85. no; 70 beats per min $\times$ 60 min per h $\times$ 24 h per day is $70 \times 60 \times 24 = 100,800$ beats per day.

86. 1 digit $\times$ 3 digits: $4 \times 300 = 1200$; 2 digits $\times$ 2 digits: $50 \times 50 = 2500$; 1 digit $\times$ 4 digits: $1 \times 1000 = 1000$

87. 42 pennies; Explanations will vary.

88. X; A zippy has an even number and a black square or triangle inside a polygon with an "antenna."

89. 8 males, 20 children

90. Detroit, 1,027,974; Flint, 140,761; Grand Rapids, 189,126; Lansing, 127,321; Warren, 144,864; Comparisons will vary.

91. about 8 ft; Explanations will vary.

93. Fill B and pour it into A, leaving 4 c in B. Empty A. Pour B into A, leaving 1 c in B. Empty A. Pour the 1 c from B into A. Fill B. Pour B into A until A is full, which takes 2 c and leaves 5 c in B.

94. row 55, column B

95. 4; Explanations will vary.

96. sphere; 13 or 21 or 49; Answers will vary.

97. 60 square feet

98. Estimates will vary.

99. Possible answers: Since 36×62 is equal to 36×52 plus 36×10, it is $1872 + 360$, or 2232; similarly, it is $2592 - 360 = 2232$. Or, since 62 is halfway between 52 and 72, the product is halfway between 1872 and 2592: since $2592 - 1872 = 720$, the product is 360 more than 1872 and 360 less than 2592.

100. Tower Y is taller; Possible explanations: Since 1 yd = 3 ft, tower Y is $41 \times 3 \times 2 = 246$ ft tall and tower Z is $2 \times 120 = 240$ ft tall. Or, tower Z is $(120 \div 3) \times 2 = 80$ yd tall and tower Y is $41 \times 2 = 82$ yd tall. The towers look the same height because of the scales; both are 2 in high, but 1 in represents a different length in each drawing.